WILD AMERICA

MOUSE

By Lee Jacobs

BLACKBIRCH®
PRESS

THOMSON
✳
GALE™

San Diego • De

JACKSON COUNTY LIBRARY SERVICES
MEDFORD, OREGON 97501
aine • London • Munich

THOMSON
GALE

For more information, contact
The Gale Group, Inc.
27500 Drake Rd.
Farmington Hills, MI 48331-3535
Or you can visit our Internet site at http://www.gale.com

Photo Credits: cover, pages 3, 4, 5, 7, 14 © Thomas Kitchin & Victoria Hurst; pages 6, 8, 9, 15, 16-17, 18-19, 20-21, 23 © CORBIS; page 10 © Glenn Vargas, California Academy of Sciences; page 11 © George W. Robinson, California Academy of Sciences; pages 12, 22 © Corel Corporation; page 16 © ArtToday

LIBRARY OF CONGRESS CATALOGING-IN-PUBLICATION DATA

Jacobs, Lee.
  Mouse / by Lee Jacobs.
    v. cm. — (Wild America series)
Includes bibliographical references.
Contents: The mouse's environment — The mouse body — Social life — The mating game — Mice and humans.
  ISBN 1-56711-569-1 (hardback : alk. paper)
  1. Mice—Juvenile literature. [1. Mice.] I. Title.
QL737.R6 J235 2003
599.35—dc21   2002011927

Printed in China
10 9 8 7 6 5 4 3 2 1

Contents

Introduction

Mice are part of a huge group of mammals called rodents. They belong to the order Rodentia. All rodents have two pairs of incisor teeth. These sharp, chisel-like teeth in the upper and lower jaw are used to gnaw and chew.

There are many different groups within order Rodentia. The largest is called Myomorpha, or mouse-like rodents.

Mice are part of the mammal group called rodents.

Five families make up Myomorpha. Four of these families are small and include some species of mice such as jerboas, dormice, and jumping mice. The fifth family—the Muridae—includes more than 95 percent of all mice and rat species. Besides mice and rats, other animals in this family are hamsters, gerbils, voles, lemmings, and mole rats.

Members of the Muridae family live in all parts of the world except Antarctica. Many species of mice live in North America, including cotton and harvest mice. (The field mouse is actually a vole.) The most common mice found in Canada and the United States are house mice and white-footed mice, or deer mice. In fact, the house mouse is thought to be the most common rodent in the world.

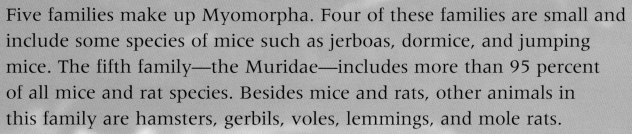

There are many species of mice in North America. The most common are house and white-footed mice.

The Mouse's Environment

As their name suggests, house mice like to stay near people. Houses, barns, and stores are all places where these mice live. They also live in farm fields where they can find food. House mice will move to the woods in warm weather. They know how to build burrows with many rooms. They can also make nests of leaves and grasses. But most house mice prefer to hole up in any spot that is cozy and close to food. They tear or chew up soft materials, such as clothes and newspapers, to make a comfortable nest.

A house mouse can chew through soft material to make a nest.

White-footed mice mainly live in the wild, in many kinds of habitats including wetlands, grasslands, forests, and deserts. They look for areas that are warm and dry. Many do not build their own nests. Instead, they take over homes that other animals leave behind. They also choose hidden spots such as tree hollows, gaps under rock ledges, and other places where they will be safe. Some white-footed mice carefully build nests of grass. Harvest mice, also found in many parts of North America, build homes that look like bird nests.

A white-footed mouse finds a home that is warm and dry.

The Mouse Body

House mice are grayish brown or gray, with undersides that are lighter in color. Some have black streaks in their fur. They are small creatures that weigh only about 1 ounce (28 g) and stand 1 inch (2.5 cm) tall. About 3 to 4 inches (8 to 10 cm) long, they have tails nearly as long as their bodies. Their long, scaly, hairless tails help them balance when they climb. Mice use their sensitive whiskers to aid their sense of touch. Whiskers help them do things such as tell if a hole is big enough to slip through.

Mice have whiskers on their faces, as well as on their legs and bodies.

A full grown mouse weighs only 1 ounce (28 g).

House mice have fuzzy vision. They cannot see more than a few inches in front of them. But their eyes are located on either side of the head, so they can see movement from several directions. Their pointy noses give them a keen sense of smell that leads them to food sources and helps them identify other mice. These mice have large rounded ears and excellent hearing. They also have glands on the bottom of their feet that leave scent trails. A house mouse can follow its trail back to the safety of its home.

Because a mouse's eyes are on either side of its head, it can see movement from many directions.

White-footed mice have light gray, dark brown, or reddish brown fur with lighter-colored undersides. They lick their fur to keep it well groomed. As their name says, their feet are white. Like house mice, they weigh about 1 ounce (28 g). They range from 3 to 6 inches (8 to 15 cm) in length, and have furry tails that vary from just 1 inch to about 9 inches (2.5 to 23 cm) long. The length of the tail depends on where the mouse lives—on the ground or in trees.

Some white-footed mice that spend a lot of time in trees need longer tails to balance and climb. White-footed mice have large ears and eyes, and have better eyesight than house mice.

Left: White-footed mice have white feet and furry tails.
Right: White-footed mice have better eyesight than house mice.

Social Life

White-footed mice are nocturnal, which means they are most active at night. Unlike house mice, white-footed mice rarely live among people. They protect their own territory and do not often live in large groups. But these mice do have ways to communicate with each other. They might leave scent marks, stamp their feet, or squeak. They will also tap on hollow stems with their front feet to spread an alarm to other mice. Mice may also communicate with high-pitched sounds that humans cannot always hear.

House mice are also nocturnal, but they can be active during the day. They live in loose family groups that may include several females and their babies. Males live in the group too, but they do not stay with one female. Females are called does, and males are called bucks. There is often one strong male mouse, or chief buck, in charge of a family.

The mice in a family group groom each other and help care for the nest. Males urinate at the boundaries to mark the territory. They also patrol each night. Fights can break out over territory.

An owl swoops down to prey upon a nocturnal white-footed mouse.

Males that are not part of the family are not allowed in, but unknown females are often welcome.

Many animals prey on mice, including owls, dogs, cats, snakes, birds, skunks, and foxes. Just about any animal that eats meat will dine on a mouse. Mice have ways to protect themselves. Their small size helps them slip away from danger into spots too small for their enemies. They also move very quickly, so they are often able to out-run or outclimb predators. Mice will even swim, if needed, to escape danger.

Food Gathering

House mice are omnivorous, which means that they eat both plants and animals. Because house mice can squeeze through tiny openings, climb, and swim, they can reach all kinds of food. Mice that live indoors will eat foods that humans leave behind, such as table scraps, cereal, chocolate, and pet food. They are quick to pick up dropped crumbs, and often find their way into kitchen cupboards. They will even eat soap! Outside, house mice mainly eat insects, as well as seeds, grains, fruits, and other plant foods.

House mice that live outdoors eat plants and insects.

House mice that live near humans do not hibernate (sleep through the winter) or store food. But those that live in the wild do build up quite a few small supplies of food. Even though they do not hibernate, house mice can go into a deep sleep called dormancy if the weather gets too cold. When they are dormant, the functions of their bodies, including their heartbeat, slow down to save energy.

White-footed mice eat grasses, seeds, and insects, as well as berries, nuts, snails, slugs, and insect larvae. They climb trees to find food. Like house mice, white-footed mice do not hibernate, but they do store food for the winter months. They carry food in their cheeks and hide it in several places near where they live.

Upper right: White-footed mice store food near where they live.
Right: A mouse prepares to eat a butterfly. Mice will eat just about anything.

15

The Mating Game

In northern regions, house mice generally breed from spring to fall. In southern regions, they breed all year. Females can reproduce from the age of 6 weeks. They give off a special scent when they are ready to mate. This attracts a male partner, which begins to chase the female. Once they mate, female house mice are pregnant for about 3 weeks before they have a litter (a group of babies born at the same time). They generally give birth about 5 times a year, but they can have up to 12 litters in a single year. An average litter has 5 or 6 baby mice, but there can be as many as 13 babies.

Right: White-footed mice collect soft material to help build their nests.
Inset: Male mice stay with females for a few days during breeding season.

White-footed mice also breed throughout the year, as long as the weather is not too cold. Males usually mate with more than one female each season. Females can reproduce from 6 or 7 weeks of age and usually have 4 or 5 litters per year. Like house mice, white-footed mice have pregnancies that last about 3 weeks. There are 2 to 9 babies in a litter. White-footed mice make birthing nests of leaves and grass lined with any soft materials they can find.

Females are very territorial during this time. The male stays with the female for a few days during breeding season, but does not stay to care for the young.

Babies

Mice babies are called pups or pinkies. They are born deaf and blind. As soon as they are born, the mother licks them clean and dries them off. Their pink bodies are hairless, but they have whiskers. The tiny pups are about half an inch (1 cm) in length and weigh less than one-quarter of an ounce (0.6 g)! Pinkies rely on their mothers for everything they need to survive. They drink their mother's milk for about 18 days. The mother keeps them warm and safe. If a predator is near, she will carry each baby to safety, one at a time, by the scruff of its neck.

Mice babies are called pinkies. They are deaf and blind when they are born.

18

A mother will even fight off a much larger animal, such as a cat, if her babies are in danger. Sometimes, female house mice from the same family group will nest together and help care for each other's young.

By the time the pups are 4 to 5 days old, their ears open. After 8 to 9 days, they grow fur. Their eyes open when they are about 2 weeks old. Within another few days, the babies start to eat solid food, but still nurse. When pups are 1 month old, they stop nursing and are ready to go out on their own. Mice that live in the wild generally have a life span of 1 to 2 years.

Left: Some female house mice nest together and help care for each other's babies.
Inset: Mice pups grow fur on their bodies after 8 to 9 days.

Mice and Humans

Wild mice generally do not interfere much with human activity. But house mice are different. These mice, which first came from Asia, reached all parts of the world when they traveled on ships with explorers and settlers. They have almost constant contact with humans, and actually depend on people to survive. House mice adapt easily to human environments, and make use of all food and shelter opportunities. At the same time, they try to avoid dangers such as mousetraps and pets.

Pet mice depend on food and shelter from humans to survive.

Many people think of mice as pests and set traps to kill them. Mice can cause a lot of damage. They chew through things, ruin food, and leave droppings everywhere. Many types of mice also spread sicknesses such as Lyme disease and hantavirus. But outdoors, mice can be good to have around. They help keep the insect and weed population down, and are an important food source for many mammals, birds, and snakes. They also scatter seeds as they eat, which aids tree and plant growth. And partly because there are so many of them, scientists use mice in studies that help them learn about diseases that humans get. Some people even keep mice as pets.

Though they are pests indoors, mice help to control weeds and insect populations outdoors.

Glossary

buck a male mouse

doe a female mouse

dormancy temporarily asleep or inactive

hibernate sleep through the winter

litter a group of babies born to one mother at the same time

nocturnal asleep during the day and active at night

omnivore an animal that eats both plants and animals

pinky a baby mouse

predator an animal that hunts other animals for food

pup a baby mouse

For Further Reading

Books

Fischer-Nagel, Heiderose, and Andreas. *A Look Through the Mouse Hole.* Minneapolis, MN: Carolrhoda Books, 1989.

Himmelman, John. *A Mouse's Life.* (Nature Upclose) Chicago, IL: Childrens Press, 2000.

Miller, Sara Swan. *Rodents: From Mice to Muskrats.* Danbury, CT: Franklin Watts, 1998.

Souza, D. M. *It's a Mouse!* Minneapolis, MN: Carolrhoda Books, 1998.

Index